Alexander Graham Bell

by Lucia Raatma

Compass Point Early Biographies

*Thank you to Sharon Morrow, Heritage Presentation Services,
Alexander Graham Bell National Historic Site of Canada,
Baddeck, Nova Scotia, Canada*

*Reading Adviser: Dr. Linda D. Labbo,
Department of Reading Education, College of Education,
The University of Georgia*

COMPASS POINT BOOKS
Minneapolis, Minnesota

Compass Point Books
3109 West 50th Street, #115
Minneapolis, MN 55410

Visit Compass Point Books on the Internet at *www.compasspointbooks.com*
or e-mail your request to *custserv@compasspointbooks.com*

Editor: Christianne C. Jones
Photo Researcher: Marcie C. Spence
Designer/Page Production: Bradfordesign, Inc./Les Tranby

Library of Congress Cataloging-in-Publication Data
Raatma, Lucia.
    Alexander Graham Bell / by Lucia Raatma.
        p. cm. — (Compass Point early biographies)
Summary: Simple text describes the life and accomplishments of scientist, inventor,
and teacher Alexander Graham Bell, who is best known for inventing the telephone.
Includes bibliographical references and index.
ISBN 0-7565-0569-0 (hardcover)
1. Bell, Alexander Graham, 1847-1922—Juvenile literature. 2. Inventors—United States—
Biography—Juvenile literature. 3. Telephone—History—Juvenile literature. [1. Bell, Alexander
Graham, 1847-1922. 2. Inventors. 3. Telephone—History.] I. Title. II. Series.
    TK6143.B4R28 2004
    621.385'092—dc22   2003012307

Table of Contents

A New Way to Communicate 5

An Interest in Sound 6

The Young Scientist 10

Teaching Speech 12

The Telephone 16

Showing the World 19

Always a Teacher 21

More Inventions 24

An Important Life 26

Important Dates in Alexander Graham Bell's Life . . 28

Glossary 29

Did You Know? 30

Want to Know More? 31

Index 32

NOTE: In this book, words that are defined in the glossary are in **bold** *the first time they appear in the text.*

A New Way to Communicate

Can you image your life without the telephone? People have telephones at work and at home. Many people also have cell phones.

In the mid-1800s, telephones didn't exist. People communicated by writing letters or sending messages by **telegraph.** The telegraph used Morse code, a series of dots and dashes **transmitted** over wires.

Alexander Graham Bell changed all that. He was interested in how people talk and communicate with one another. His work led to the development of the telephone.

◄ Alexander Graham Bell in the early 1900s

Bell at age 11

An Interest in Sound

Alexander Graham Bell was born in Edinburgh, Scotland, on March 3, 1847. Bell's name was passed on from his grandfather and his father. Many people called him Alec.

As he grew up, Bell learned skills from both of his parents. His father, Alexander Melville Bell, helped people improve their speech. He created a sound alphabet made

Bell (far right) with his family near Edinburgh, Scotland

of pictures. These pictures were called visible speech. Bell and his two brothers helped their father with his work.

Although his mother, Eliza Bell, was almost deaf, she was still a talented musician. She was also an artist. Like his mother, Bell enjoyed playing the piano and was a fine musician.

Bell's grandfather was also interested in helping people improve their speech. In 1862, Bell spent one year with his grandfather in London, England. He was close to his grandfather and enjoyed learning from him.

In 1863, Bell began teaching music and speech at Weston House Academy. It was a boys' school near Edinburgh, Scotland. Bell taught in exchange for classes, food, and a

Bell with his grandfather (left) and his father

place to stay. He studied at the University of Edinburgh in 1864. He used his education and knowledge of visible speech to become a teacher of the deaf in 1868.

9

The Young Scientist

When Bell was in his early 20s, he began working on experiments to figure out how people produced vowel sounds. Hermann von Helmholtz, a German scientist, was also working on this.

Von Helmholtz used electric **tuning forks** to make vowel sounds. Bell was interested in his work. Von Helmholtz's experiments gave Bell the idea that electricity could be used in some way to send speech.

Hermann von Helmholtz

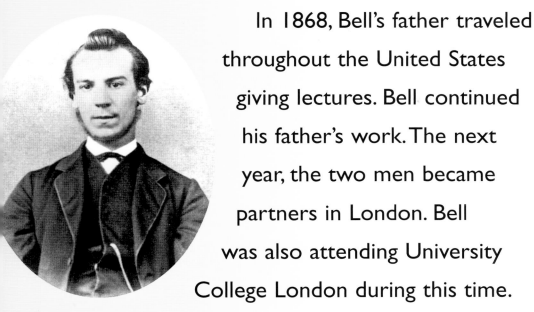

Bell in the mid-1860s

In 1868, Bell's father traveled throughout the United States giving lectures. Bell continued his father's work. The next year, the two men became partners in London. Bell was also attending University College London during this time.

The following years were sad ones for Bell. His two brothers died from **tuberculosis,** and he became sick as well. Bell's father left his work in London, and the family moved to Brantford, Ontario, in Canada. His parents hoped that the weather in Brantford would be better for Bell's health.

11

Teaching Speech

Shortly after the Bell family moved to Canada, Sarah Fuller approached Bell and his father. She worked at a school for deaf people in Boston, Massachusetts. Sarah was interested in visible speech. She hoped that Bell or his father would show her teachers how to use it.

In 1872, Bell moved to Boston and opened a school for teachers of the deaf. He became a professor at Boston University the next year.

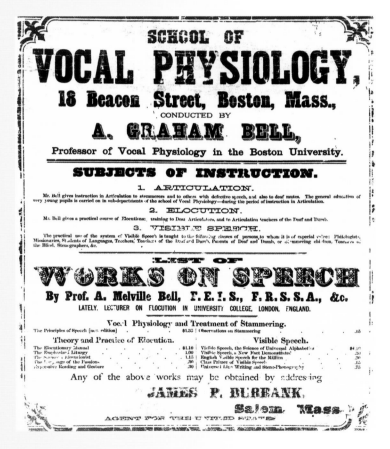

SCHOOL OF
VOCAL PHYSIOLOGY,
18 Beacon Street, Boston, Mass.,
CONDUCTED BY
A. GRAHAM BELL,
Professor of Vocal Physiology in the Boston University.

SUBJECTS OF INSTRUCTION.
1. ARTICULATION.

Mr. Bell gives instruction in Articulation to stammerers and to others with defective speech, and also to deaf mutes. The general education of very young pupils is carried on in sub-departments of the school of Vocal Physiology—during the period of instruction in Articulation.

2. ELOCUTION.

Mr. Bell gives a practical course of Elocution: training to Deaf Articulators, and to Articulation teachers of the Deaf and Dumb.

3. VISIBLE SPEECH.

The practical use of the system of Visible Speech is taught to the following classes of persons to whom it is of especial value: Philologists, Missionaries, Students of Languages, Teachers, Teachers of the Deaf and Dumb, Parents of Deaf and Dumb, or stammering children, Teachers of the Blind, Stenographers, &c.

LIST OF
WORKS ON SPEECH
By Prof. A. Melville Bell, F.E.I.S., F.R.S.S.A., &c.
LATELY, LECTURER ON ELOCUTION IN UNIVERSITY COLLEGE, LONDON, ENGLAND.

Vocal Physiology and Treatment of Stammering.

The Principles of Speech [new edition] . . $1.35 | Observations on Stammering 15

Theory and Practice of Elocution.		Visible Speech.	
The Elocutionary Manual	$1.10	Visible Speech, the Science of Universal Alphabetics	$4.00
The Emphasized Liturgy	1.00	Visible Speech, a New Fact Demonstrated	.50
The Science of Elocutionist	1.15	English Visible Speech for the Million	.30
The Language of the Passions	.30	Class Primer of Visible Speech	.15
Expressive Reading and Gesture	.30	Universal Line Writing and Steno-Photography	.75

Any of the above works may be obtained by addressing
JAMES P. BURBANK,
Salem, Mass.
AGENT FOR THE UNITED STATES.

An advertisement promoting one of Bell's classes at Boston University

Bell (top right) and his students at the Boston School for the Deaf

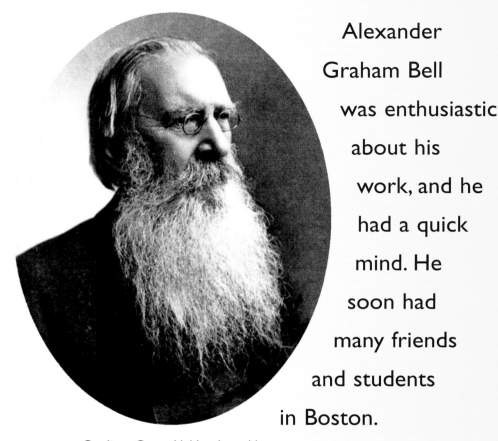

Alexander Graham Bell was enthusiastic about his work, and he had a quick mind. He soon had many friends and students in Boston.

Gardiner Green Hubbard would become Bell's father-in-law.

One student was Mabel Hubbard. She would later become Bell's wife. Mabel had lost her hearing as a child. Mabel's father, Gardiner Green Hubbard, was grateful for the help Bell was giving his daughter. He was also interested in Bell's ideas for improving the telegraph. Hubbard offered Bell money to continue his work with the telegraph.

Bell loved the time he spent teaching his students. He did telegraph experiments in his spare time. At first, he did not try to send speech by electricity. Instead, he tried to send several telegraph messages over the same wire at one time.

Because he was busy teaching, Bell soon realized he needed help on his experiments. Thomas Watson began working as Bell's assistant. The two men became good friends.

The Telephone

Bell and Watson performed countless experiments with the telegraph. During the summer of 1875, they spent hours working in the laboratory. They made changes to the telegraph, which allowed human voices to be heard through the wires.

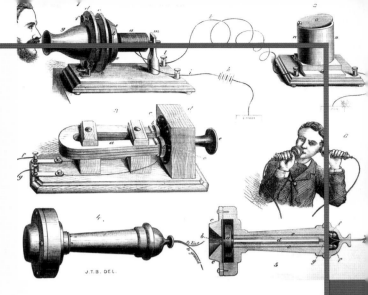

On March 10, 1876, Alexander Graham Bell transmitted human speech for the first time. He was 29

Detailed diagram showing how Bell's phone worked

years old. Bell and Watson were in different rooms and were trying a new type of transmitter. Watson heard Bell say, "Mr. Watson, come here. I want to see you." Those were the first words ever heard over a telephone!

Although Bell had a **patent,** he may not have been the original inventor of the telephone. In 2002, Congress named Italian-American inventor Antonio Meucci the official

◄ A painting of Bell and Watson in the laboratory around 1887

Antonio Meucci

inventor of the telephone.

Antonio Meucci lived in New York and had a one-year **caveat** on his version of the telephone. However, he could not afford to renew it after the year was up.

In 1875, Bell wrote the details for getting a patent for his version of the telephone. In March of the next year, the patent was awarded to Bell. He received full credit as the inventor of the telephone in the United States until 2002. Other countries still recognize Bell as the official inventor.

18

Bell showed his telephone to people all over the world. ➤

Showing the World

In June 1876, Bell showed his telephone at the Centennial Exposition in Philadelphia, Pennsylvania. The judges were impressed by Bell's new machine. The British scientist Sir William Thomson called the telephone "the most wonderful thing in America."

In the years to come, Bell and Watson showed the telephone to many people. Their work eventually made telephone service possible in the United States. The the first telephone company, the Bell Telephone Company, was formed on July 9, 1877.

The Implement of the Nation

AMERICAN TELEPHONE & TELEGRAPH CO.
LOCAL AND LONG DISTANCE TELEPHONE
BELL SYSTEM AND ASSOCIATED COMPANIES

SECRETARY of War Stanton sat in his office in Washington.

"If I ring that bell," he said, "any man, *in the most distant State*, is a prisoner of war!"

The telephone bell has succeeded the messenger bell.

Business has succeeded war.

If *any man* in the Union rings the bell of his Bell Telephone at his desk, any other man *at the most distant point* is at his instant command.

That is the Bell Companies' ideal—that you may take the receiver off the hook and get into communication with *any man*, even in the most distant State.

That is the really *universal telephone* that the Bell Companies set as their goal at the beginning. It is so far realized that already 20,000,000 voices are at the other end of the line, all reached by the one Bell system.

The *increased efficiency* of the individual, of the lawyer or bank president or corporation official; the increased efficiency of the *nation as a whole*, because of the development of the Bell system, can hardly be estimated.

It certainly *cannot* be overestimated.

The president of a corporation to-day could not be the president of such a corporation without it.

The modern corporation *itself* could not exist without telephone service of national scope.

Corporation officials could not have transacted business quickly enough by old methods to reach the totals which alone are accountable for our remarkable commercial development as a nation.

The wheels of commerce have been kept at the necessary speed to provide this swift development by the universal telephone.

The mere item of *time actually saved* by those who use the telephone means an *immense increase* in the production of the nation's wealth every working day in the year.

Without counting the convenience, without counting this wonderful increased efficiency, but just counting *the time alone*, over *$3,000,000* a day is saved by the users of the telephone!

Which means *adding $3,000,000 a day to the nation's wealth!*

The exchange connections of the associated Bell Companies are about 18,000,000 a day—the toll connections half a million more. Half of the connections are on business matters that must have prompt action—either a messenger or a personal visit.

Figured on the most conservative basis, the money value of the *time saved* is not less than ten cents on every exchange connection and three dollars on every toll, or long distance connection—figures that experience has shown to be extremely low.

The saving *in time only* is thus $1,800,000 daily on exchange messages and $1,500,000 on long distance messages—this much added to the nation's productiveness by the Implement of the Nation, the Bell Telephone.

American Telephone & Telegraph Company

The American Telephone & Telegraph Company, known as AT&T, was originally part of the Bell Telephone Company.

Always a Teacher

Only two days after
the Bell Telephone
Company was
created, Alexander
Graham Bell and
Mabel Hubbard

Alexander Graham Bell family

were married. They traveled to England and
showed people the telephone.

In May 1878, their daughter Elsie was
born in England. They moved to Washington,
D.C., that November. Their daughter Marian
was born there in 1880.

Teacher and student demonstrating one of Bell's inventions

Bell chose not to work in the telephone business. Instead, he continued to be a teacher.

In 1880, Bell received the Volta Prize from France for the telephone. He used the prize money to help create the Volta Laboratory.

In 1890, Bell founded the American Association to Promote the Teaching of Speech to the Deaf. Today, the association is called the Alexander Graham Bell Association for the Deaf and Hard of Hearing.

Helen Keller (left), who was deaf and blind, and her teacher Annie Sullivan were good friends with Bell.

More Inventions

Bell continued to invent things for the rest of his life. He invented an electric **probe** that helped doctors find bullets in the human body. His machine was used in surgery before the X-ray was introduced. It was like a metal detector.

Bell was also interested in flying. Many scientists were working on similar ideas. The Wright brothers had the first successful flight

Men demonstrating Bell's kite

Bell (second from right) worked closely with members of the Aerial Experiment Association. The AEA included members from the United States and Canada.

in 1903. Bell helped American scientist Samuel P. Langley in his experiments with flying machines. Bell also performed his own flying experiments with kites.

In 1907, Bell and his wife helped organize the Aerial Experiment Association in Canada. This group worked to make improvements in **aviation**. Bell also helped create *Science* magazine and helped organize the National Geographic Society.

An Important Life

In January 1915, Bell made the first telephone call across the United States. He was in New York, and he called Thomas Watson in San Francisco. Bell spoke those famous words: "Mr. Watson, come here. I want to see you." Watson laughed and said the trip might take awhile.

Bell spent most of his later life at his Canadian home on Cape Breton Island, Nova Scotia. He worked in his laboratory, played

Bell (middle) answered questions after he made the first telephone call across the United States.

Bell continued to work all his life.

piano, and enjoyed his family and friends. He died in Nova Scotia on August 2, 1922. Every telephone in the United States was silent for one minute to honor him. The silence was a fitting tribute to a man who helped bring sound to everyone.

Important Dates in
Alexander Graham Bell's Life

1847	Born on March 3 in Edinburgh, Scotland
1863	Teaches and attends classes at Weston House Academy
1864	Attends the University of Edinburgh, Scotland
1868	Teaches speech to deaf children; attends University College London
1870	After the death of his brothers, moves to Canada with his family
1872	Moves to Boston to teach at a school for deaf children
1874	Works on the telephone; meets Thomas Watson
1876	Receives a patent and, on March 10, speaks the first words over the telephone; shows the telephone at the Centennial Exposition in Philadelphia that summer
1877	Founds the Bell Telephone Company; marries Mabel Hubbard on July 11
1915	Makes the first telephone call across the United States
1922	Dies on August 2 in Nova Scotia, Canada

Glossary

aviation—the science of building and flying aircraft

caveat—a written description of an invention that is good for one year

patent—a legal document that gives an inventor the right to make and produce an item

probe—a tool used to explore something

telegraph—a system that uses wires and codes to send messages over long distances

transmitted—sent from one place to another, usually as a form of communication

tuberculosis—a serious bacterial disease that affects the lungs

tuning forks—pieces of metal with prongs that are used to tune musical instruments; when struck, the tuning forks vibrate and produce a specific tone

Did You Know?

- Bell didn't have a middle name until 1858. He adopted his middle name out of admiration for family friend Alexander Graham. From then on, his full name was Alexander Graham Bell.

- In 1878, Rutherford B. Hayes became the first U. S. president to have a telephone installed in the White House. The first person he called was Alexander Graham Bell.

- In 1882, Alexander Graham Bell became a citizen of the United States.

- President James A. Garfield was shot in 1881 and later died. Bell was called in to use his electric probe to try to locate the bullet. However, the alarm kept going off no matter where Bell put the probe. People later realized that the metal springs in Garfield's mattress caused the alarm to go off.

Want to Know More?

At the Library

Ford, Carin T. *Alexander Graham Bell: Inventor of the Telephone.*
Berkeley Heights, N.J.: Enslow, 2002.

Linder, Greg. *Alexander Graham Bell: A Photo-Illustrated Biography.*
Mankato, Minn.: Bridgestone Books, 1999.

Mara, Wil. *Alexander Graham Bell.* Danbury, Conn.: Children's Press, 2002.

Shuter, Jane. *Alexander Graham Bell.* Portsmouth, N.H.: Heinemann, 2000.

On the Web

For more information on *Alexander Graham Bell,* use
FactHound to track down Web sites related to this book.

1. Go to *http://www.compasspointbooks.com/facthound*
2. Type in this book ID: 0756505690
3. Click on the *Fetch It* button.

Your trusty FactHound will fetch the best Web sites for you!

Through the Mail

**Alexander Graham Bell Association
for the Deaf and Hard of Hearing**
3417 Volta Place, N.W.
Washington, DC 20007
To write for more information about this
organization's mission and history

On the Road

Alexander Graham Bell National Historic Site of Canada
P.O. Box 159
Baddeck, Nova Scotia B0E IB0
Canada
To visit the museum that tells the story of Bell's life

Index

Bell, Alexander Graham, *4, 11, 12, 16, 19, 23, 25, 26, 27*
    birth of, 6
    childhood of, *6, 7, 7, 9*
    death of, 27
    education of, 8–9
    marriage of, 21
    teaching career of, 8–9, *12,* 13, *13,* 22
Bell, Alexander Melville (father), 6–7, *7, 9,* 11
Bell, Eliza (mother), 7, 8
Bell, Elsie (daughter), 21, *21*
Bell, Mabel (wife), 14–15, 21, *21,* 25
Bell, Marian (daughter), 21, *21*
Bell Telephone Company, 20, *20*
Boston, Massachusetts, 12, *12,* 13, 14
Boston School for the Deaf, *12*
Boston University, 13, *13*
Brantford, Ontario, 11
Cape Breton Island, Nova Scotia, 26–27
Centennial Exposition, 19, *19*
Edinburgh, Scotland, 6, 8
Fuller, Sarah, 12
grandfather, 8, *9*
von Helmholtz, Hermann, *10,* 10
Hubbard, Gardiner Green, 14–15, *14*
Hubbard, Mabel. *See* Bell, Mabel.
Keller, Helen, *23*
kite, *24,* 25
Langley, Samuel P., 25
London, England, 8, 11
Meucci, Antonio, 17–18, *18*
Morse code, 5
Philadelphia, Pennsylvania, 19
Sullivan, Annie, *23*
telegraph, 5, 15, 16
telephone, 5, 17, *17,* 18, 19, *19,* 20, 26, *26*
University College London, 11
University of Edinburgh, 9
visible speech, 7, 9, 12
Washington, D.C., 21
Watson, Thomas, 15, 16, *16,* 17, 20, 26
Weston House Academy, 8

About the Author

Lucia Raatma received her bachelor's degree in English literature from the University of South Carolina and her master's degree in cinema studies from New York University. She has written a wide range of books for young people. When she is not researching or writing, she enjoys going to movies, practicing yoga, and spending time with her husband, daughter, and golden retriever. She lives in New York.